Agency Creation- R. 3d "Agency is the fiduciary relationship that arises when one person manifests assent to another person that the agent shall act on the principles behalf and subject to the principles control and the agent manifests assent or otherwise consents to act"

Creation of actual authority- 1. An objective manifestation by principal 2. Followed by A's reasonable interpretation of that manifestation 3. Which leads A to believe that is authorized to act for P

I. **Doctrine of inherent power**- For agency to exist the P must manifest consent to have A act on P's behalf with respect to some goal, task, or set of responsibilities

A. **Actual authority**- 2 flavors, Express/

implied… Express- Conferred by words, writing, specifying agents authority.. Implied- A GM purchasing widgets for a business

B. **Apparent-** 3rd party believes that A has authority of P to act on their behalf. 3rd party reasonably believes that they have actual authority… Ex:

Art collector sending employee to buys something & auction house believes the A has actual authority.

C. Rowen case-

Doctrine of inherent power, electric company was suing landlord, tenant had no actual authority to exceed the 45k limit. Not apparent authority to create agency by estoppel, there was no reliance on a disclosed principal. When there is no disclosed principal/reliance, the last opportunity is the **doctrine of inherent power**- you can recover against would be p for act of would be A if the agent is acting within their scope of **inherent**

power.. LL tenant doesn’t create an agency relationship. No general agent = no inherent power to bind a would be P for an unauthorized act. At most tenant was a special agent, no inherent power, electrical company out of luck

D. Healthcare v Royal healthcare- Implied Actual authority, nursing home management group, vs an insurance co. Entering the picture is a subcontractor. Whether nursing home must pay for services provided, mgmt. company ran out of money and the court said the nursing home had to pay. K between nursing home and management said <u>"nothing in this agreement shall be meant to construe agency/fiduciary duty"</u> Home had no contact with service provider, management had no authority to bind the nursing home. Court ruled there is no apparent authority, service provider dealt with manager (existing prior relationship) No reasonable belief they were dealing with someone to act/ bind someone else.. You cant have implied actual authority in the face of secret instructions. Management had an ongoing relationship with nursing home, the agreement struck with service provider was within the scope of their inherent power..

II. **Agency by Estoppel-** Someone doesn't have actual authority & the agent induces a 3rd party

Estoppel- 1. The person intentionally or carelessly caused such belief

2. Having notice of such belief and that it might induce others to change their positions the person didn't take reasonable steps to notify them of the facts

Hoddison- *Agency by estoppel*- customer in a furniture store, met by a shadowy guy at the door. Furniture never arrived, store had no record of the sale. Guy wasn’t an employee, gave the appearance that he was a store employee. PERCEPTION of customer, there was nothing that would reasonably suggest that this guy was not authorized to act on behalf of store. <u>No facts that this guys authorization was attributable to the store</u> (2nd ingredient of agency by estoppel, would be P didn’t do anything to stop the would be agent)

<u>Agency by estoppel-</u> 2nd element is a neglect/failure to act. (comes in flavor of someone purporting to act on their behalf with a 3rd party, and find out in time to prevent any harm to third party, & they have an opportunity to stop the act and fail to do so) Other type of neglect, “you are responsible by your own

neglect by creating the situation that these folks found themselves in”.. Can’t run a store in such a way where someone can pretend to be an agent, transact business, & disappear. **NEGLECT**

Right for agent to bind P only exists with Actual authority (express/implied) Implied would be anything reasonably necessary/appropriate in carrying out what you have the actual authority to do. EX: if you're the president of a company then you can do certain things

Special agency only applies if **undisclosed principal**

General employee ordering supplies for his employer (ex GM, etc)

1. **Frolic-** deviations that pose risks of harm of a type significantly different than the types inherent in the servants task.
2. **Detour-** considered within the scope of employment.. (ex 2 people making a delivery and stopping at a store for a sandwich)

Misrepresentation by an agent or apparent agent- Principal will be liable to third party if 1. A person has actual or apparent authority to make statements concerning a particular subject 2. The person makes a misstatement of fact concerning that subject 3. A third party relies on that misstatement and 4. The third party suffers physical harm as a result. EX: Construction manager supervising a building sends a prospective tenant to an unsafe stairwell… (owner is liable)

III. **<u>Attribution rule</u>**- if an agent acting within scope of actual/apparent authority makes a misstatement they are attributable to the principal for K law.. EX: a law school dean making misrepresentations about their school being accredited and not. The dean is attributable to the law school

A. **Robichaud Case**- Borrower, bankteller, bank. Got a 2000$ 10/year loan. Insurance Co only covered loans that were 10 yrs or less. Teller checked a book said they have ins. Court held bank liable for remaining balance. (they didn't actually have insurance) Teller didn't have any actual authority, but had apparent authority. Her actions were <u>attributable</u> to the bank,.. They believed the teller had authority to check the records, this appearance is attributable to the bank. Nothing in bank suggested they should go elsewhere besides the teller to confirm there is insurance. T

Second element of apparent authority- belief must be based on apparent authority attributable to the principal.

B. **Eliot case**- guy applied for a job, met with VP in Dallas. Understanding was that he would be hired for 1 yr and would be able to work in Georgia. Employee reported to work in Dallas & VP told him he had to move to Dallas.

(job was contingent upon this) Plaintiff even said under oath “he didn’t think the VP had authority to make decision”, but the VP was his only contact, and he did believe that when VP came back at a later time saying he was hired, he thought the VP had the ability to report the decision made by higher up Attributable to the company by appearance

Ratification- When a P affirms a previously unauthorized act. It validates the original unauthorized act and produces the same legal consequence as if original act was authorized

A. Preconditions- There must be an unauthorized transaction

B. Affirmance- A purported principal

ratifies by either manifesting/engaging

IV. **Ratification**- When a P affirms a previously unauthorized act. It validates the original unauthorized act and produces the same legal consequence as if original act was authorized

Preconditions- There must be an unauthorized transaction

Affirmance- A purported principal ratifies by either manifesting/engaging

Perkins v Rich- **implied ratification based upon conduct of would be p**Minister borrowed $ to make improvements, the committee never took notice of the ministers conduct. “committees knowledge of substantial improvements at the church should have provoked an investigation to lead to the discovery of the mortgages"... They were getting the **benefit of the deal**, by seeing improvements being made and never inquired to where the cash was coming from.... (why not apparent authority—because 3rd party is a bank, banks know minister doesn't have authority to do this) No reasonable belief that minister had this type of power,

John sexton & co- Deals with tortious misrepresentation by an agent. Officers for a co promised lifetime employment. Respondeat superior theory,

Inherent power- undisclosed principal... If

disclosed- apparent authority & estoppel

Demian Ltd v Frank- importer didn't send stuff the way it was supposed to come through, importer sued the middleman (broker)... Is broker liable for someones failure to perform (if party down the line is brokers agent= then liable, if the party down the line is the importers agent= there is no liability) **General vs special agent**.. Middle man got away because in the contract there was a provision guaranteeing performance to the principal & then it became irrelevant if Frank would be responsible

Ell Dee clothing co v Marsh- There was no insurance company. AN insurance broker had been doing business for years & never had a problem. Agent didn’t know that policies would go to a clubhouse, and theyd bid on the policy. (insurer and broker had no clue about this) Before policy was picked up by a club member, there was a loss (before the insurance was bound) Agent was acting on good faith, technically there was no insurance. **When you have an undisclosed/partially disclosed P**, the AGENT is liable When P falls through for no reason the client has any control over, A is liable, even when acting in good faith... There was no P here

Resnick v Abner- client co/advertising co.

State of knowledge of the 3rd party is a factual issue... Court says what the 3rd party knew, should have know will determine the outcome... *Mere presence of a name doesn't make the principal disclosed...*

Grinder v Bryans- Actual agency, **ELECTION** rule-you can sue party you dealt with, or their principal once you discover there is one (elect between party you dealt with or their p) Case stands for when your dealing 1 on 1 with someone, and you find out after the fact that they were acting for someone else, you have a claim against the party you were dealing with. If they met the req for inherent power, then you have a claim against the remote party..

Ins co of North America v Miller- enumerates all the duties of principals to agents.. Particular duty that an A may not acquire any benefit from the performance of their agency, without express knowledge or approval of the principal

Southern farm casualty v Allen- Agent knew of the brothers putting ins in different name, the knowledge isn't imputed to the principal if an agent goes rogue, and starts colluding against their principal(and the third party knew it), they are no longer an agent

Sutton Mutual Ins co v Notre Dame- Ins co, Hockey arena, President..

Must notify ins co if there is a claim, or have reason to know there might be a claim. The pres of the arena saw this, and argument is that the pres knowledge should be imputed to the arena. He wasn’t acting in his capacity as pres at the time incident occurred, he also didn’t know it would be his obligation to report. If you don’t know you had to pass on the info then its not imputed

Georgia pacific & great plains bag co-

Laches.. once you know someone is stepping on your toes and your gonna complain about it, do it within a reasonable time... Company knew of the other using their trademark, court determines what knowledge will/wont be imputed... EX: warehouse people not imputed, but higher level=yes it is imputed

Lane Mortgage v Crenshaw- Non-agency/quasi situations... Power coupled with an interest is different, tenant could rent out space in return for money he lent to owners.. Owners sold the company, the brought in new managing agent.. The new agent terminated him, he was agent until entire mortgage was paid off. Court ruled this wasn't actual agency, the managing agent had a power coupled with an interest.

Power coupled- one party gives another party power to act in their place, in return for some underlying interest. Until underlying interest Is satisfied power cannot be removed

i. Generally,

t
h
e

r
e
l
a
t
i
o
n
s
h
i
p

o
f

e
m
p
l
o
y
e
r

a
n
d

e
m
p
l
o
y
e
e

e
x
i
s
t
s

w
h
e
n

t
h
e

p
e
r
s
o
n

f
o
r

w
h
o
m

t
h
e

s
e

r
v
i
c
e
s

a
r
e

p
e
r
f
o

r
m
e
d

h
a
s

t
h
e

r
i
g

h
t
t
o

d
i
r
e
c
t
a
n
d

c

o
n
t
r
o
l
t
h
e

m
e
t
h
o
d

a
n
d

m
a
n
n
e
r

i
n

w

h
i
c
h

t
h
e

w
o
r
k

s
h

a
l
l
b
e

d
o
n
e

a
n
d

t

h
e

r
e
s
u
l
t
t
o

b
e

a

c
c
o
m
p
l
i
s
h
e
d
,
w
h
i
l

e

a
n

i
n
d
e
p
e
n
d
e
n
t

c
o
n
t
r
a
c
t
o
r

i
s

o
n

e

w
h
o

e
n
g
a
g
e
s

t
o

p
e
r
f
o
r
m

s
e
r
v
i
c
e

s

f
o
r

a
n
o
t
h
e
r

a
c

c
o
r
d
i
n
g

t
o

h
i
s

o

w
n

m
e
t
h
o
d

a
n
d

m
a

n
n
e
r
,
f
r
e
e

f
r
o
m

d

i
r
e
c
t
i
o
n

a
n
d

c
o
n

t
r
o
l
o
f

t
h
e

e
m
p
l
o

y
e
r

i
n

a
l
l
m
a
t
t
e
r

s

r
e
l
a
t
i
n
g

t
o

t
h

e

p
e
r
f
o
r
m
a
n
c
e

o
f

the work, except

a
s

t
o

t
h
e

r
e
s
u
l
t

o
r

t
h
e

p
r
o
d
u
c
t
o
f

his work.[FN11]

ii.

iii. F
N
1
1
.
O
t
h
e
r

f
a
c
t

o
r
s

t
h
a
t
m
a
y

b
e

c

o
n
s
i
d
e
r
e
d

i
n
c
l
u
d

e
:
(
1
)

t
h
e

s
u
b
s
t
a

n
t
i
a
l
i
t
y

o
f

t
h
e

i
n
v
e
s
t
m
e
n
t
o
f

t
h
e

p
e
r
s
o
n

r
e
n
d
e
r
i
n

g

t
h
e

s
e
r
v
i
c
e

i
n

his own tools a

n
d

e
q
u
i
p
m
e
n
t
;
(
2
)

t
h
e

c
o
s
t
i
n
c
u
r
r
e

d
b
y
t
h
e
a
l
l
e
g
e
d

e m p l o y e e i n r e n

d
e
r
i
n
g

t
h
e

s
e
r
v
i

c
e
,
a
s

b
y

t
h
e

e
m
p

loyment of his ow

n

l
a
b
o
r
e
r
s
;
(
3
)

t

h
e

a
b
i
l
i
t
y

o
f

t
h

e

p
e
r
s
o
n

r
e
n
d
e
r
i

n
g

t
h
e

s
e
r
v
i
c
e

t

o

p
r
o
f
i
t

f
r
o
m

h
i
s

o
w
n

"
m
a
n
a
g
e
m
e
n
t

skill"; (4) wheth

e
r

o
r

n
o
t
t
h
e

s
e
r

v
i
c
e

i
n
v
o
l
v
e
d

r
e

quires a special

s
k
i
l
l
;
(
5
)

t
h
e

p
e

r
m
a
n
e
n
c
y

o
f

t
h
e

r
e
l
a
t
i
o
n
s
h
i
p

b
e
t

w
e
e
n

t
h
e

p
a
r
t
i
e
s

; and (6) whether

t
h
e

p
e
r
s
o
n

r
e
n
d

e
r
i
n
g

t
h
e

s
e
r
v
i
c

e

w
o
r
k
s

i
n

t
h
e

c

o
u
r
s
e

o
f

t
h
e

r
e
c

i p i e n t ' s

b u s i n e s

s

r
a
t
h
e
r

t
h
a
n

i
n

a
n

a
n
c
i
l
l
a
r
y

c
a

p
a
c
i
t
y
.
A
v
i
s

R
e
n
t

A Car System, Inc

. v . United States

, 503 F.2d 423, 42

9 (2d Cir. 1974).

The concepts of apparent authority, and agency by estoppel are closely related. Both depend on manifestations by the alleged principal to a third person, and reasonable belief by the third person that the alleged agent is authorized to bind the principal. The manifestations of the principal may be made directly to the third person, or may be made to the community, by signs or advertising. Restatement (Second), Agency §§ 8, 8B, 27 (1957). In order for the third person to recover against the principal, he must have relied on the indicia of authority originated by the principal

a three-prong test under general agency law in order to determine the existence of apparent agency: first, whether there was a representation by the principal; second, whether a third party relied on that representation; and, finally, whether the third party changed position in reliance upon the representation and suffered detriment.

Class 2/11

#7 Drummond v Hilton

i. P

l
a
i
n
t
i
f
f
'
s

c
o
n
t
e

n
t
i
o
n

t
h
a
t
H
i
l
t
o
n

s
h
o
u
l
d

b
e

l
i
a
b
l

e

f
o
r

t
h
e

a
l
l
e
g
e

d

n
e
g
l
i
g
e
n
t
a
c
t
s

o
f

C
r
e
a
t
i
v
e
,
i
r
r
e

s
p
e
c
t
i
v
e

o
f

a
n

a

c
t
u
a
l
a
g
e
n
c
y

r
e
l
a

t
i
o
n
s
h
i
p
,
i
s

b
a
s
e

d

o
n

t
h
e

d
o
c
t
r
i
n

e

o
f

a
p
p
a
r
e
n
t
a
g
e

n
c
y

a
s

s
e
t
f
o
r
t
h

b
y

t
h
e

R
e
s
t
a
t
e
m
e

n
t
(
S
e
c
o
n
d
)

o
f

A
g

e
n
c
y

s

2
6
7

(
1
9
7
5

), which provides

a
s

f
o
l
l
o
w
s
:
ii. O
n
e

w
h
o

r
e
p
r
e
s
e
n
t
s

t

h
a
t

a
n
o
t
h
e
r

i
s

h

i
s

s
e
r
v
a
n
t

o
r

o
t

h
e
r

a
g
e
n
t

a
n
d

t
h

e
r
e
b
y

c
a
u
s
e
s

a

t

h
i
r
d

p
e
r
s
o
n

j
u
s
t

i
f
i
a
b
l
y

t
o

r
e
l
y

u
p
o
n

t
h
e

c
a
r
e

o
r

s
k
i
l
l

o
f

s
u
c
h

a

p
p
a
r
e
n
t

a
g
e
n
t

i
s

s
u
b
j
e
c
t

t
o

l
i
a
b

i
l
i
t
y

t
o

t
h
e

t
h
i

r
d

p
e
r
s
o
n

f
o
r

h
a

r
m

c
a
u
s
e
d

b
y

t
h
e

l
a
c
k

o
f

c
a
r
e

o
r

s
k
i
l
l

o
f

t
h
e

o
n

e

a
p
p
e
a
r
i
n
g

t
o

b

e

a

s
e
r
v
a
n
t

o
r

o

ther agent as if

h e w e r e s u c h .

Boyd v Lumber-

Respondeat Superior,

Workmans comp case. They were determining if employee/ind contractor. RS- 1. Employment status 2. Scope of employmentRIGHT TO CONTROL "They had the right to control the manner and means by which the work was done" <<<< This establishes master/servant relationship

ACTUAL CONTROL-

Marvel- IRS Taxation; employee(employer must withhold taxes) vs ind contractor (taxed themselves)Employers must withhold tax money for gov for their employees; not for ICs.. Analyzed through the “right to control the manner and means by which work is done" analysis.

Cowen- "did the remote party have the ability to control how the police officers did their job"

Davila- Was the intentional tort committed within the reasonably foreseeable range of activities within their job? Was this within the scope of employment? Remanded back to the factfinder for this determination

Good v Berrie-

Frolic/detour.. Employment status non-issue, he stopped and went to a baseball game.. Court found he was within scope of employment, he was on a detour

Gizzi v Texaco-

Apparent Servant Doctrine… Doesn't matter with what the appearance of servant status is, this is another type of "quasi estoppel".. Common to all apparent servant cases is you have 1 party that for a profit, leads another party to rely on them to trust the quality of repair, etc. Service station paid franchise fees; person trusts quality of work at station and is injured as a result of this trust.. *Inducing another party for profit, rely on 3rd party, injured as a result(and disclaiming liability when they do get hurt)*

Drumond v Hilton Hotel- Apparent servant doctrine applied beyond the service station; citing *Gizzi v Texaco*, court talked about master/servant relationship; Test whether the would be master has the right to exercise control over the manner and means by which the would be servant does its work. **The more the franchise agreement dictates how stuff is done, the closer it**

comes to making the franchisee the servant of the franchisor...

Different example: Franchisor markets the hotel as being very safe, someone is robbed in the lobby because they believed it was safe/secure, victim goes expecting degree of safety, they might be able to make the case for res sup or app servant doctrine.

Mullen v Horton- Apparent servant doctrine Priest sleeping with client; she brings suit under *respondeat superior*.. He was working for the counseling office when this happened. **Intentional misconduct is usually outside the scope of employment**. Church induced victims trust... Connecticut hasn't yet recognized the Apparent servant doctrine

Ramos v Preferred Mecical- Apparent servant scope, 2 parents, sick son, 2 Drs, HMO... HMO was liable for alleged misdeeds of doctors in HMO that aren't employees

LP/GP/LLP/LLLP/ Dissolution

Dissolution- 1. Caused by expiration of the partnership term/accomplishment of the partnership undertaking, **2.** The will of a partner (rightfully if partnership is at will; wrongfully if in contravention of the partnership agreement) **3.** Mutual assent of all partners, **4.** Expulsion of a partner **5.** Illegality of the partnership of death or bankruptcy of a partner; or **5.** A court order because of incompetency of a partner, unprofitability, etc...

- Duty to wind up the partnership's affairs.. If wrongful the partners may have action for damages
- Assets distributed to creditors who aren't

partners, then partner creditors, then to partners to return capital contributions and finally to partners for proportional share of their profits.

- Does not terminate the partnership

Partners always have the power, not the right to terminate

Can be by acts of the parties: Agreement, by will of partner, mutual assent, expulsion of partner

Operation of law: illegality, death, bankruptcy

Decree of Court: incompetency, incapability, improper conduct, business operating only at a loss, circumstances rendering dissolution equitable

If dissolution violates the agreement there is a right to

damages, right to purchase the business (need to post a bond/ failure to pay can result in compensation to other partner)

Death: Surviving partner must act as a fiduciary in liquidating the partnership and must account to deceased partner for the value of their interest in partnership. (continuing business without consent/delay = unjustified)

Surviving partner gets compensation for services in winding down the partnership

Winding up- The process of settling affairs after dissolution. Only transactions designated to terminate are within the scope of partners actual authority.

Liability for false statements in a LP- if 1.Any person who signed knowing it contained a false statement and 2. Any GP who knew/should have known that the certificate contained a false statement

LLC- Provides owners with two main features: 1. Limited liability that shareholders of a corporation enjoy 2. Tax advantages that partners enjoy

- Automatically taxed as a partnership unless it

elects to be taxed as a corporation

- Profits and losses shared based on the value of members contributions

www.ingramcontent.com/pod-product-compliance
Lightning Source LLC
Chambersburg PA
CBHW031629210526
45464CB00004B/1821
9781728694764